MEDICAL BREAKTHROUGHS

THE FIRST HEART TRANSPLANT

A GRAPHIC HISTORY

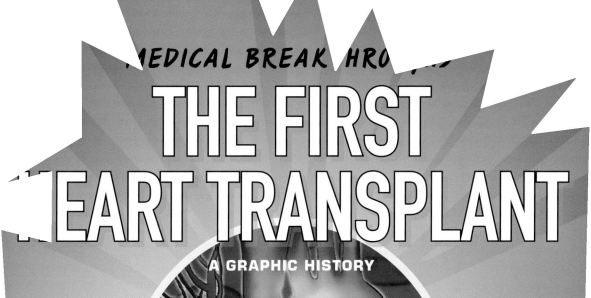

BRANDON TERRELL

ILLUSTRATED BY DANTE GINEVRA

GRAPHIC UNIVERSE™ • MINNEAPOLIS

T0018826

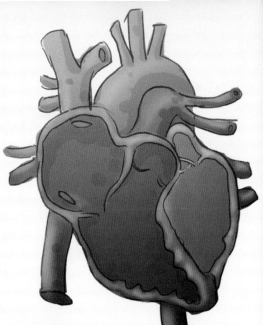

Brandon M. Terrell (1978–2021) was a talented storyteller, authoring more than one hundred books for children. He was a passionate reader, Star Wars enthusiast, amazing father, and devoted husband. This book is dedicated in his memory—happy reading!

Graphic Universe™
An imprint of Lerner Publishing Group, Inc.
241 First Avenue North
Minneapolis, MN 55401 USA

For reading levels and more information, look up this title at www.lernerbooks.com.

Main body text is set in Dave Gibbons Lower. Typeface provided by Comicraft.

Library of Congress Cataloging-in-Publication Data

Names: Terrell, Brandon, 1978-2021 author. | Ginevra, Dante, 1976- illustrator.
Title: The first heart transplant : a graphic history / Brandon Terrell ; illustrations by Dante Ginevra.
Description: Minneapolis : Graphic Universe, [2022] | Series: Medical breakthroughs | Includes bibliographical references and index. | Audience: Ages 8–12 | Audience: Grades 4–6 | Summary: "For centuries, people misunderstood how the heart works. Even as organ transplants became more common, heart transplants remained dangerous. But small groups of pioneering doctors attempted this difficult surgery, changing the lives of patients"— Provided by publisher.
Identifiers: LCCN 2021014445 (print) | LCCN 2021014446 (ebook) | ISBN 9781541581531 (library binding) | ISBN 9781728448701 (paperback) | ISBN 9781728444130 (ebook)
Subjects: LCSH: Heart—Transplantation—Juvenile literature. | Transplantation of organs, tissues, etc.—Juvenile literature.
Classification: LCC RD598.35.T7 T47 2022 (print) | LCC RD598.35.T7 (ebook) | DDC 617.4/120592—dc23

LC record available at https://lccn.loc.gov/2021014445
LC ebook record available at https://lccn.loc.gov/2021014446

Manufactured in the United States of America
1 – CG – 12/15/21

TABLE OF CONTENTS

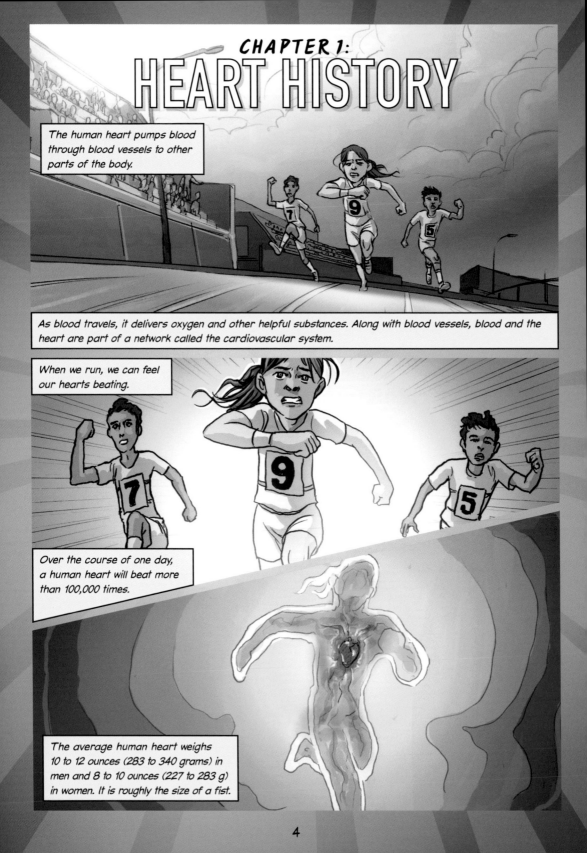

CHAPTER 1:
HEART HISTORY

The human heart pumps blood through blood vessels to other parts of the body.

As blood travels, it delivers oxygen and other helpful substances. Along with blood vessels, blood and the heart are part of a network called the cardiovascular system.

When we run, we can feel our hearts beating.

Over the course of one day, a human heart will beat more than 100,000 times.

The average human heart weighs 10 to 12 ounces (283 to 340 grams) in men and 8 to 10 ounces (227 to 283 g) in women. It is roughly the size of a fist.

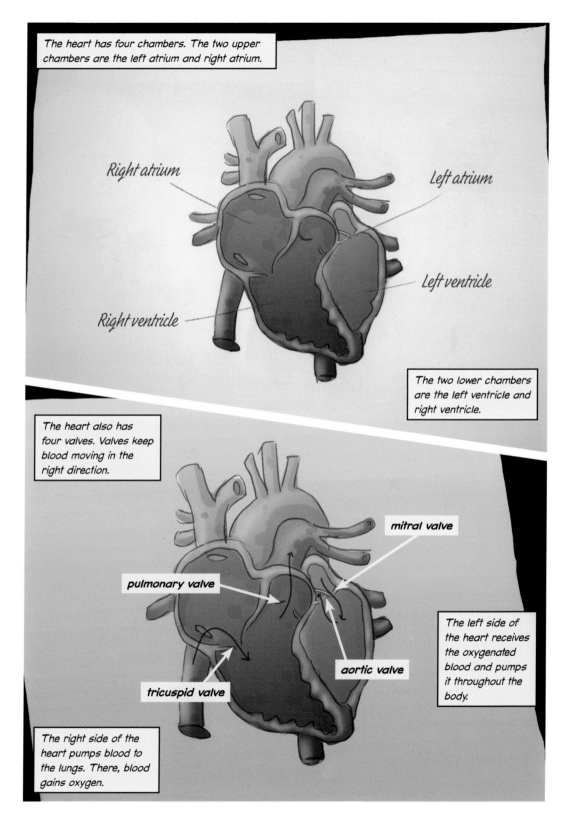

The heart has four chambers. The two upper chambers are the left atrium and right atrium.

Right atrium

Left atrium

Left ventricle

Right ventricle

The two lower chambers are the left ventricle and right ventricle.

The heart also has four valves. Valves keep blood moving in the right direction.

mitral valve

pulmonary valve

The left side of the heart receives the oxygenated blood and pumps it throughout the body.

aortic valve

tricuspid valve

The right side of the heart pumps blood to the lungs. There, blood gains oxygen.

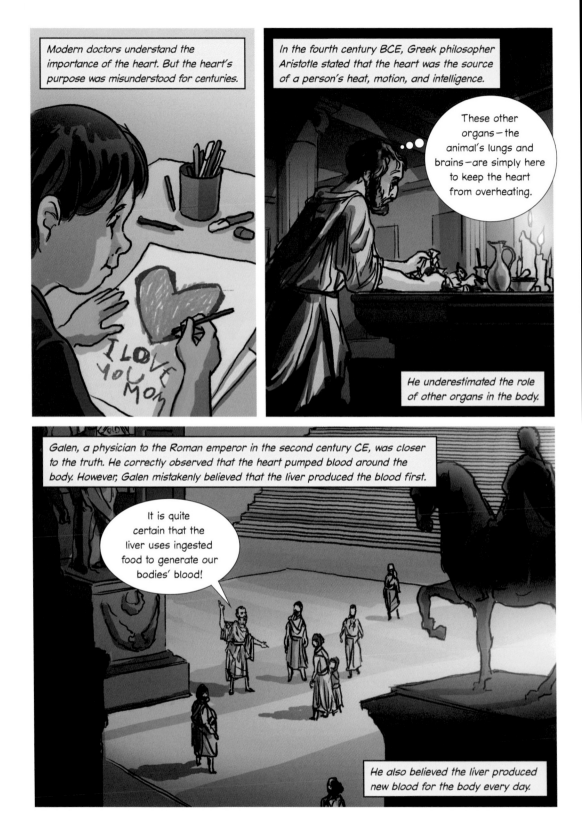

Modern doctors understand the importance of the heart. But the heart's purpose was misunderstood for centuries.

In the fourth century BCE, Greek philosopher Aristotle stated that the heart was the source of a person's heat, motion, and intelligence.

These other organs—the animal's lungs and brains—are simply here to keep the heart from overheating.

He underestimated the role of other organs in the body.

Galen, a physician to the Roman emperor in the second century CE, was closer to the truth. He correctly observed that the heart pumped blood around the body. However, Galen mistakenly believed that the liver produced the blood first.

It is quite certain that the liver uses ingested food to generate our bodies' blood!

He also believed the liver produced new blood for the body every day.

People trusted Galen's theories for centuries. But in the mid-1600s, scientist William Harvey challenged Galen's belief that the body created new blood daily. Harvey measured the volume of blood that the heart pumped around the body.

This is simply too much to produce each day!

In 1628, Harvey published his findings in his work Anatomical Studies on the Motion of the Heart and Blood.

So, humans have a limited blood supply?

Yes, it's constantly circulating!

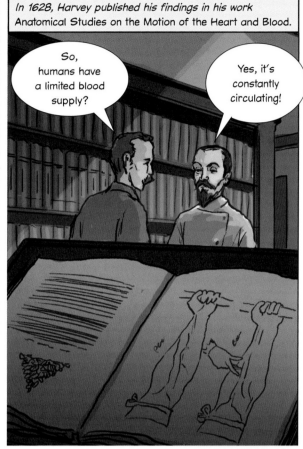

By the 1800s, doctors understood the anatomy and function of the heart very well. Nonetheless, the medical community advised against heart surgery because it was so dangerous.

Some doctors continued to push the boundaries of medicine. In 1893, a fight in Chicago, Illinois, would lead to one of the most daring surgeries of its time.

8

Dr. Williams worked hard to save Cornish's life. He carefully cut through nerves, muscles, and blood vessels, creating a small trapdoor leading to the heart. This opening let Williams reach Cornish's wound.

Scalpel, please.

Williams stitched closed a severed artery. He also closed a wound in the sac surrounding Cornish's heart. Then, Williams sewed Cornish's chest back up.

The hospital discharged Cornish several weeks later. The press hailed the operation as a major success.

Thanks, Dr. Williams.

In the twentieth century, Chicago became a training ground for physicians who wanted to push the boundaries of medicine.

This would lead to many more daring surgeries, including organ transplants.

CHAPTER 2:
TRANSPLANT SCIENCE

In 1951, inventor and physician Dr. Adrian Kantrowitz produced the first film showing the inside of a beating heart. The footage helped the medical community better understand the heart's valves and other inner workings.

Soon after, surgeon John H. Gibbon Jr. developed a device known as a heart-lung machine. The heart-lung machine could do the work of the heart and lungs during surgeries. This allowed for longer surgery times, as the machine maintained the circulation of blood and oxygen within a patient's body.

In 1953, Dr. Henry Swan II also discovered a way to give surgeons more time. He began safely inducing hypothermia in patients.

The cooling slows the body's metabolism. That stops the brain from needing as much oxygen and allows us to safely stop the heart.

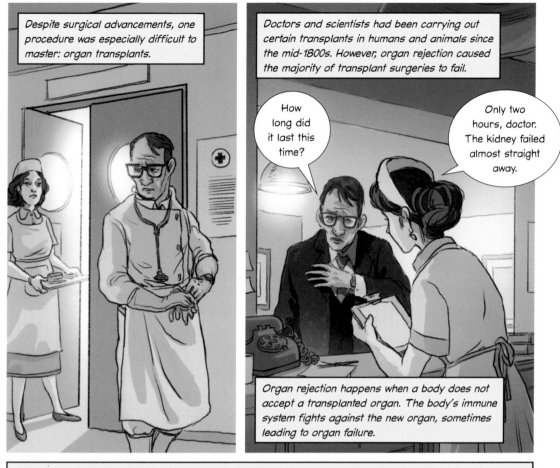

Despite surgical advancements, one procedure was especially difficult to master: organ transplants.

Doctors and scientists had been carrying out certain transplants in humans and animals since the mid-1800s. However, organ rejection caused the majority of transplant surgeries to fail.

How long did it last this time?

Only two hours, doctor. The kidney failed almost straight away.

Organ rejection happens when a body does not accept a transplanted organ. The body's immune system fights against the new organ, sometimes leading to organ failure.

In the early 1950s, scientists conducted a study on skin grafts in cows. The study confirmed that fraternal and identical twin cows almost never rejected their twin's organs.

This finding marked a hopeful new chapter in human transplant surgeries. It began with identical twin brothers Richard and Ronald Herrick.

In the summer of 1953, Richard Herrick fell ill while serving a tour of duty around the Great Lakes.

Doctor, I'd give him one of my own kidneys if it would help?

I'm sorry, Mr. Herrick. You have chronic nephritis, an infection that leads to kidney failure. There's nothing we can do to help you.

The Herrick twins were transferred to Peter Bent Brigham Hospital in Massachusetts. There, they underwent a series of tests to prepare for transplant surgery. The build-up attracted national media attention.

Doctors are preparing twin brothers Richard and Ronald Herrick for kidney transplant surgery.

On December 23, 1954, the brothers' operations took place. In one room, doctors removed the failing kidney from Richard. In the other, a healthy kidney was carefully taken from Ronald.

12

The team of doctors, led by Dr. Joseph E. Murray, worked for hours. When the new kidney was in place, the team waited to see if it had worked.

The operation was a success! Richard Herrick became the first human organ transplant survivor.

Herrick lived for another eight years. However, his chronic nephritis returned in 1962, and he died from the illness that same year. His brother Ronald lived for 56 more years after the surgery.

Surgeons soon carried out other successful organ transplants in humans. The first pancreas transplant occurred in 1966, and the first liver transplant in 1967.

liver

pancreas

Then, also in 1967, transplant surgeries took a giant step forward with the first heart transplant.

CHAPTER 3:
THE FIRST HEART TRANSPLANT

In 1958, Dr. Norman E. Shumway joined the faculty at the Stanford University School of Medicine in California.

At Stanford, Shumway researched heart transplantation in animals such as dogs.

Dr. Richard Lower assisted Shumway in this work. For almost a decade, Shumway and Lower studied heart transplantation. Then, in 1967, Shumway decided to attempt the surgery in humans.

It's risky, but we have to try.

On November 20, 1967, Shumway announced his intentions to the press.

Failing hearts need to be replaced with healthy hearts. And that is why I will be attempting the first human heart transplant, as soon as a donor is available.

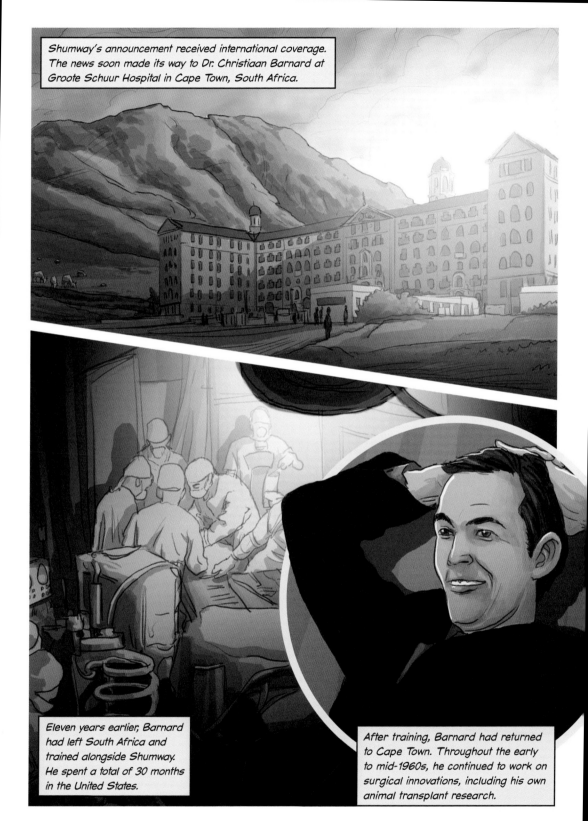

Shumway's announcement received international coverage. The news soon made its way to Dr. Christiaan Barnard at Groote Schuur Hospital in Cape Town, South Africa.

Eleven years earlier, Barnard had left South Africa and trained alongside Shumway. He spent a total of 30 months in the United States.

After training, Barnard had returned to Cape Town. Throughout the early to mid-1960s, he continued to work on surgical innovations, including his own animal transplant research.

At the time Shumway made his announcement, Barnard felt that he too was ready to carry out a heart transplant. He asked the Groote Schuur Hospital's professor of cardiology, Dr. Velva Schrire, if he knew of an appropriate patient.

Did you find anybody?

I have a patient who may be a good subject for your surgery, doctor.

The patient's name was Louis Washkansky. Washkansky was 53 years old and had suffered severe heart failure from heart disease.

Yes, let's do the surgery. It's the only way for me to live.

Next, Dr. Barnard needed a donor heart.

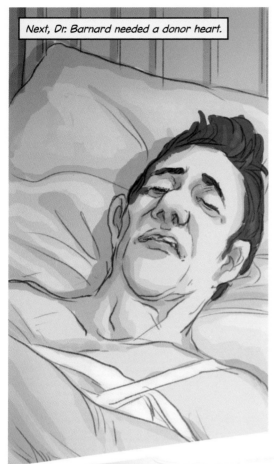

The donor's name was Denise Darvall. On the afternoon of December 2, 1967, 25-year-old Darvall was in a traffic accident.

At Groote Schuur Hospital, medics declared Darvall brain-dead from the incident. But Darvall's father allowed Dr. Barnard to use her still-beating heart for his transplant surgery.

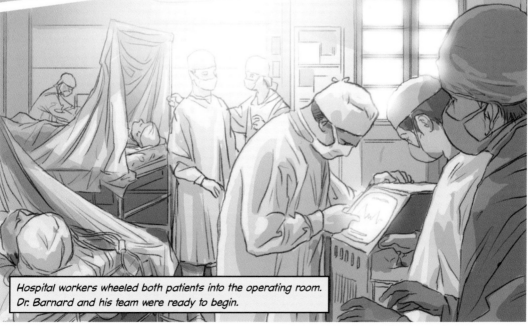

Hospital workers wheeled both patients into the operating room. Dr. Barnard and his team were ready to begin.

Barnard's team included his brother, Marius Barnard. Marius had assisted Christiaan during previous transplant attempts in dogs.

But some members of Barnard's surgical team had never seen or carried out a heart transplant in their lives!

All right, everyone. Let's begin.

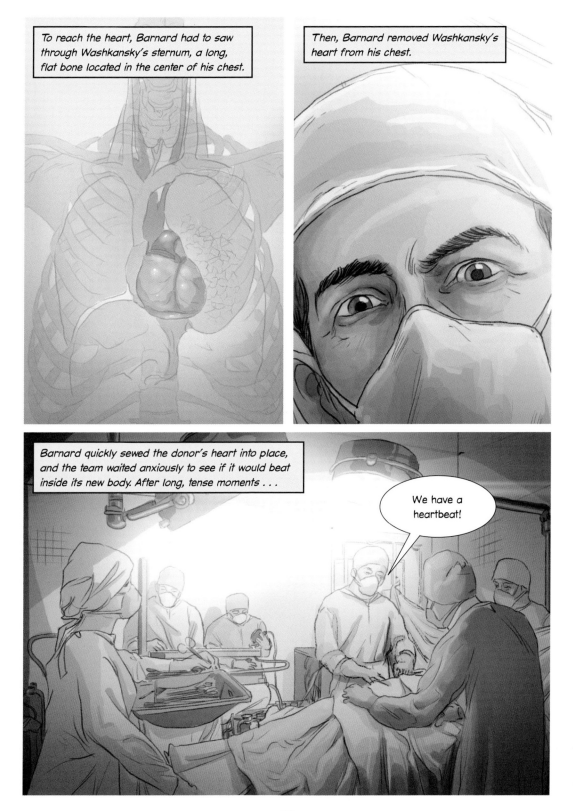

To reach the heart, Barnard had to saw through Washkansky's sternum, a long, flat bone located in the center of his chest.

Then, Barnard removed Washkansky's heart from his chest.

Barnard quickly sewed the donor's heart into place, and the team waited anxiously to see if it would beat inside its new body. After long, tense moments . . .

We have a heartbeat!

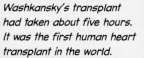

Washkansky's transplant had taken about five hours. It was the first human heart transplant in the world.

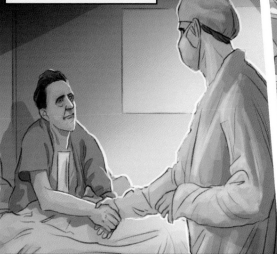

News of the operation spread rapidly. Within one hour, even the Prime Minister of South Africa knew of the transplant.

Washkansky's recovery became a global story. Photographers and reporters flew in to glimpse the suddenly famous patient.

Meanwhile, in the United States, Dr. Shumway was readying his own heart transplant surgery. As he prepared for the operation, he felt relieved that Barnard was distracting the media.

Excellent. Let Christiaan have the limelight. I'll simply remain focused on my work.

At first, Washkansky recovered well. For the first time in medical history, doctors were able to observe the positive effect of a transplanted heart.

However, Washkansky soon fell ill. Eighteen days after the surgery, he died.

Just weeks after Dr. Barnard's surgery in South Africa, Dr. Shumway found somebody in need of a new heart.

The man's name was Mike Kasperak. Kasperak was a steel worker with terminal heart disease.

Kasperak and his wife, Ferne, decided that surgery was their only option.

Should I go ahead with it?

I want you alive with me.

All Kasperak needed was a healthy donor heart.

In early January 1968, staff at a nearby hospital informed Shumway of a possible donor.

In a coma, you say?

Yes, after a severe brain injury. Her name is Virginia-Mae White.

Shumway quickly alerted his operating staff of the upcoming surgery.

What's that? We've got a donor? I'll be right there!

A local reporter overheard the news and spread the word. Shumway wasn't able to avoid media attention after all!

The operation lasted three and a half hours. When the donor heart began to beat in Kasperak's chest, excitement washed over the room.

It was the first successful adult heart transplant in the United States, and the fourth human heart transplant attempt in the world.

The morning after the surgery, Shumway spoke at a news conference.

We have reached first base, so to speak, but our work is just beginning.

22

After the surgery, Kasperak was alert and seemed to be on the road to recovery. He was even writing notes to his wife.

However, Kasperak had been ill at the time of the surgery, which made the recovery more difficult. He passed away two weeks after the transplant.

After Kasperak's death, Dr. Shumway continued to pioneer heart transplant practices. He was one of very few surgeons to keep carrying out this difficult surgery.

In South Africa, Dr. Barnard also continued heart transplant surgeries. His second patient lived almost 19 months after the transplant. His fifth and sixth transplant patients lived another 13 years and 23 years, respectively!

Together, the efforts of Shumway and Barnard marked a huge leap in medicine.

CHAPTER 4:
HOW THE HEART BEATS

Organ rejection and infection meant most early transplant patients did not survive, even after the transplant surgeries were successful.

Dr. Shumway spent later years researching methods to prevent organ rejection.

Other scientists were also developing tools and techniques to reduce the need for heart transplants in the first place.

This is a partial mechanical heart. It's a device that will work alongside the heart to boost blood flow.

In 1966, Dr. Adrian Kantrowitz had implanted an invention called a booster heart into a human for the first time.

And American inventor Wilson Greatbatch had patented the first internal pacemaker device in 1962.

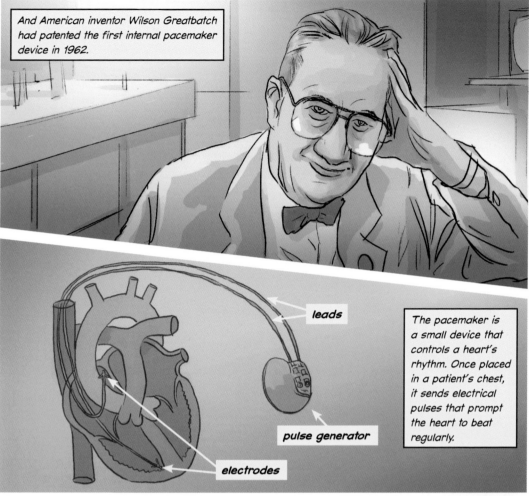

leads

The pacemaker is a small device that controls a heart's rhythm. Once placed in a patient's chest, it sends electrical pulses that prompt the heart to beat regularly.

pulse generator

electrodes

Dr. Shumway's work continued alongside these advancements. By 1991, he led the world in both the number of hearts transplanted and patient success rates.

Shumway's department performed 687 transplants in 615 patients. More than 80 percent of the patients lived longer than five years. The longest period of survival was twenty years.

By 2008, doctors in the United States were performing about 2,000 heart transplants a year.

Unfortunately, this number still falls short of the 3,500 to 4,000 people waiting for a heart or a heart-and-lung transplant at any time.

Of these people, more than 25 percent will not survive long enough to receive a donor heart.

Artificial hearts may delay the need for organ donors. Surgeons have begun to implant artificial hearts into humans as replacement organs.

The Jarvik-7 artificial heart arrived in 1982. It was the first artificial heart to be implanted in a human. The Jarvik-7 connected to a huge machine, so patients using the device could not leave the hospital.

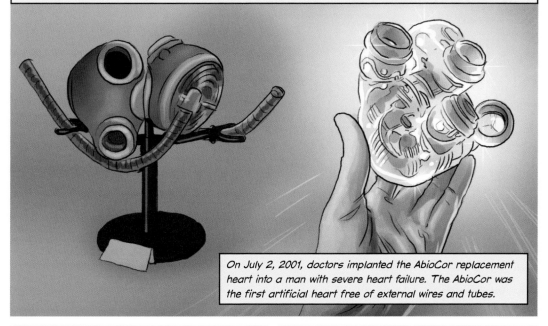

On July 2, 2001, doctors implanted the AbioCor replacement heart into a man with severe heart failure. The AbioCor was the first artificial heart free of external wires and tubes.

Scientists and physicians are also pushing the boundaries of heart transplantation using 3D printing.

A bioprinting 3D printer uses living cells—also known as bioink—to create living tissues. In 2019, scientists at Tel Aviv University in Israel took cells and other biological materials from a patient to create the world's first 3D-printed heart!

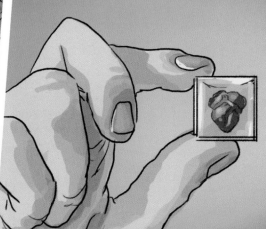

The heart was tiny. But it was the first biologically printed heart to have blood vessels and chambers. The event showed the possibility of creating perfect new hearts for specific patients.

SOURCE NOTES

21–22 Tracie White, "50 Years Ago, Stanford Heart Doctors Made History," *Stanford Medicine News Center,* January 4, 2018, https://med.stanford.edu/news /all-news/2018/01/50-years-ago-stanford-heart -doctors-made-history.html.

GLOSSARY

artery: a blood vessel that carries blood from the heart through the body

brain-dead: when a person's brain no longer functions

cardiology: the branch of medicine dealing with the heart and its diseases

circulate: to follow a course that returns to the starting point

fraternal twin: either member of a pair of twins produced from different eggs. Fraternal twins may not have the same sex or appearance.

hypothermia: a condition in which the temperature of your body is very low

immune system: the system that protects your body from diseases and infections

infection: the invasion of the body by harmful microorganisms

metabolism: a set of chemical reactions that occur in the body, such as converting food to energy

oxygenated: combined or supplied with oxygen

patent: to obtain the sole right to make or sell a product for a certain period of time

pioneer: to be the first to develop or apply an idea

severed: detached by cutting

skin graft: skin transplant surgery, or the piece of skin that is transplanted

survive: to remain alive

terminal: incurable and leading to death

FURTHER INFORMATION

Britannica Kids—Transplant
https://kids.britannica.com/kids/article/transplant/390865

Ducksters—Biology for Kids—Cardiovascular System
https://www.ducksters.com/science/blood_and_the_heart.php

Farndon, John. *Stickmen's Guide to Your Beating Heart*. Minneapolis: Hungry Tomato, 2018.

Lowe, Alexander. *Adventures in the Circulatory System*. Chicago: Norwood House Press, 2020.

Marquardt, Meg. *Discover Cutting-Edge Medicine*. Minneapolis: Lerner Publications, 2017.

YouTube—TED-Ed—How the Heart Actually Pumps Blood—Edmond Hui
https://www.youtube.com/watch?v=ruM4Xxhx32U&ab_channel=TED-Ed

INDEX